Building a Police Force
"for the good" in DR Congo
Questions that still haunt reformers and reform beneficiaries

Thierry Nlandu Mayamba

The Nordic Africa Institute
2013

NAI Policy Dialogue is a series of short reports on policy relevant issues concerning Africa today. Aimed at professionals working within aid agencies, ministries of foreign affairs, NGOs and media, these reports aim to inform the public debate and to generate input in the sphere of policymaking. The writers are researchers and scholars engaged in African issues from several disciplinary points of departure. Most have an institutional connection to the Nordic Africa Institute or its research networks. The reports are internally endorsed and reviewed externally.

Indexing terms
Congo DR
Police
Armed forces
Security sector reform
Administrative reform
Organizational change
Civil rights

The opinions expressed in this volume are those of the authors and do not necessarily reflect the views of Nordiska Afrikainsitutet.

Language checking: Peter Colenbrander
Cover photo: Radio Okapi / Ph. John Bompengo
ISSN 1654-6709
ISBN 978-91-7106-745-6
© The authors and Nordiska Afrikainstitutet 2013
Production: Byrå4
Print on demand, Lightning Source UK Ltd.

Table of contents

About the author 5

Abbreviations and acronyms 6

Introduction 7

I. Police reform: a must 9

    I.1. PdP reform: guiding principles 11

    I.2. "Police de Proximité " or "Community policing"? 12

    I.3. reform problems to overcome 14

    I.4. Donors' vs. Congolese police expectations 14

II. The winds of change 16

    II.1. 2011: another police legal establishment 16

    II.2. Implementation calendar 18

    II.3. Recruitment and territorial deployment 19

    II.4. Police personnel rejuvenation 21

    II.5. equipment acquisition and Training 22

    II.6. Improving living and working conditions 24

III. Partners and resources in police reform 27

    III.1. Normative resources 27

    III.2. international financial resources 27

    III.3. National financial resources 28

    III.4. Lobbying resources 28

IV. Main police reform partners 30

    IV.I. international reform partners 30

    IV.2. International partners trapped by reforms 31

    IV.3. what reform expects from government 34

    IV.4. when impunity undermines justice reform 36

    IV.5. Beyond facade democracy 37

V. Contemplating civil society's roles 39

    V.1. a new citizenship for a different police 40

    V.2. Debating civil-police relations 40

VI. Measuring effects 43

VII. to conclude: what next? 45

Bibliography 47

In loving memory of

Floribert Chebeya
Jacques Ebenga
Floribert Kayembe
François Kandolo

About the author

Thierry Nlandu Mayamba is Professor of English literature in the Faculty of Arts, University of Kinshasa. Dr Nlandu Mayamba received his PhD from the University of Leuven, Belgium in 1985 and since 1991 has been a professor at the University of Kinshasa.

Dr Nlandu Mayamba has also coordinated the Social Science Research Council's project on displaced children and recruitment in the Congo (2004), been a visiting scholar in visual arts and political activism at the Massachusetts Institute of Technology (2007), and contributed to the EA-SSAPR Police Reform Project (2010). In the spring of 2013, he was a guest researcher at the Nordic Africa Institute, Sweden.

Dr Nlandu Mayamba is a dramatist and is known as a political activist. His recent publications include *Du Zaïre au Congo Démocratique. Une plume pour une transition en folie?* Publibook: Paris 2006; "La musique Congolaise: entre le mirroir/cassé et recollé," in Bob W. Whyte and Lye M. Yoka (eds), *Musique populaire et Société à Kinshasa*, Harmattan: Paris 2010; and *Mapping Police Services in the Democratic Republic of Congo: Institutional Interactions at Central, Provincial and Local Levels*, IDS Research Report No. 71, 2012.

Abbreviations and acronyms

AFDL	*Alliance des Forces Démocratiques pour la Libération du Congo*
ANR	Agence National de Renseignement
CSRP	*Comité pour le Suivi de la Réforme de la Police*
DAI	Development Assistance Inc.
DFID	Department for International Development, UK
DGM	*Direction Générale des Migrations*
DRC	Democratic Republic of Congo
EA	External Accountability
EUPOL	European Union Police
EUSEC	EU Advisory and Assistance Mission for Security Reform in the DR Congo
FAZ	*Forces Armées Zaïroises*
FARDC	Forces armées de la RD Congo
GMRRR	*Groupe Mixte de Réflexion sur la Réforme et la Réorganisation de la Police*
GTS	*Groupe Technique Stratégique*
IDASA	Institute for Democracy in Africa
IDS	Institute of Development Studies
IGA	Inspection Générale de l'Audit
ISS	Institute for SecurityStudies
M23	*Mouvement du 23 Mars*
M&E	Monitoring & Evaluation
MONUSCO	*Mission des Nations Unies pour la Stabilisation du Congo*
NGO	Non-Governmental Organisation
OECD	Organisation for Economic Cooperation and Development
PdP	*Police de Proximité*
PNC	*Police Nationale Congolaise*
RRSSJ	*Réseau de la Société Civile pour la Réforme du Secteur deSécurité et Justice*
SSAPR	Security Sector Accountability and Police Reform Programme
UNDP	United Nations Development Programme

Introduction

Much has been said about the constraints facing the police reform agenda in DRC. Specialists involved in the reform process insist on the negative effects of the political allegiances of the police force on recruitment procedures, management, administration and promotion. They all note how the progressive and regular interference in the neutrality of the police force lowers ethical standards and morale, contributes to the breakdown of discipline and encourages corruption.

Experts frequently report that the political environment has strongly influenced and eroded the Congolese people's confidence in the police force, an institution that is said to attract only mediocre recruits.[1]

To the constraints mentioned above, specialists add numerous abuses such as the militarisation of the police, the devolution of its responsibilities to other agencies, the lack of resources and infrastructure, the lack of opportunities for promotion and structured training, arbitrary transfers, untimely retirements and poor remuneration and social benefits, all of which lower the collective morale of the police force.

Indeed, morphologically, the national police force is a heterogeneous force, a blend of former officers from various backgrounds: ex-FAZ, including retired officers; members of ex-militia groups; ex-military personnel; even a few widows and orphans of deceased military and police officers and educated or illiterate volunteers.[2]

The ex-combatants were integrated into the police as a matter of political convenience and without specific training. They are the beneficiaries of the permanent demilitarisation process and the restoration of peace that started in 2003 and is still proceeding.[3]

This non-professional, atypical combination of forces, a mixture of civilians and ex-military personnel of diverse origin, cannot be conducive to cohesion within the police. It results in a geographical and ethnic disequilibrium in the recruitment of police officers, in total violation of constitutional stipulations.

Finally, the variability of Congolese police agents represents a permanent threat to the people and even to the government they are supposed to protect.

---

1 Nlandu Mayamba (2012b). See p. 21 on the populace's attitudes vis-à-vis police officials.
2 Ebenga and Nlandu (2005).
3 For a more detailed discussion, see Eriksson Baaz and Verweijen (2013a); Eriksson Baaz (date?); Van Woudenberg and Shepherd (2013); Wolters (2004).

The police in DRC are indeed a permanent domestic risk. The lack of policy, service or management regime for the acquisition of equipment explains the PNC's deficient, dilapidated, obsolete and very often inappropriate equipment. The means of communication are also outdated and inadequate. Basic facilities are deficient and run down, sometimes even nonexistent.

As has become painfully clear during my research, police units have very weak operational capacity and police officers and rank-and-file lack self-confidence and pride in their profession. These shabbily dressed men and women in faded uniforms daily develop an indifferent attitude towards their profession and work in general. Inefficient and ineffective, the Congolese police force is wholly demoralised and unprofessional. Its image is that of a run-down force pervaded by corrupt villains who regularly jeopardise public confidence in the force.

To conclude, the above image has negatively affected the relationship between police and population. It has led to the withdrawal of people's cooperation, a must for successful police work and for meeting people's expectations.

I. Police reform: a must

The issue of police reform is crucial to the process of re-founding the Democratic Republic of Congo or, more accurately, to the passage from authoritarian regime to democratic one. To be effective, police reform will have to include the nationwide security systems aimed at protecting citizens and promoting the rule of law, namely, the army, the intelligence service, migration agencies and justice.

Implementing such crucial reform demands a strong political will, and regularly rethinking the existing operational framework within which questions about where and how external actors can assist reform are assessed and relevant answers are found at each step. This framework should be guided by sustainability, cohesion and relevance, to avoid repeating those reforms that did not endure and very often failed once external support came to an end.

Finally, successful police reform will raise the question of how far police institutions can be reformed in a state that has only a facade of democracy and refuses wider relevant reforms. Obviously, the police reform process in DRC will require time, resources and strong political will, all of which, unfortunately, are currently in short supply in DRC.

The present study is an attempt to produce a research outline that is intended to influence the police reform process in DRC. It is my intention to develop an analysis that responds to Congolese research priorities and perspectives, advances the process of police sector reform and facilitates engagement with the minister of the interior and security, parliament and other actors. Indeed, with regard to the police reform agenda in DRC, the time has come for all partners involved in this challenging enterprise to focus on the strategic approaches that will help engender change.

The policy dialogue is based on in-depth interviews with elite and ordinary Congolese national, regional, and local actors involved in police reform. Their opinions and comments following the publication of the report published in 2002 by the Institute of Development Studies in London[4] raised a set of practical questions related to the political and institutional environment that could stop the downward spiral of police institutions in DRC and contribute to their transformation.

Various other secondary sources were consulted for this analysis. These include the document produced by the Congolese civil society network (RRSSJ)

---

4   Nlandu Mayamba (2012c) .

on the Congolese people's vision of the police they want to create, different lobbying activity reports issued by members of the RRSSJ network, the police reform plan, laws promulgated and draft laws still under debate in parliament and stimulating research papers produced by civilians on security sector reform in DRC, with a particular focus on the police.[5]

The success of the present police reform process lies in the vision of a new police service shared by most of the stakeholders, namely, the population, the main beneficiary of police reform; the political actors who should comply with legal instruments; and the police officers and troops who are responsible for the management in the field of the police services.

Actually, all partners in the reform process officially agree on the need to implement police reform that meets to the expectations of the Congolese people it ought to protect. But for such crucial reform to succeed, a plan based on priority axes of intervention is needed. Such axes include establishing a regulatory framework to implement the organic law; stimulating civil-police relations grounded on mutual trust; developing a sound civic education programme addressing the people; elaborating police training programmes on values, ethics and police ethos; promoting the Congolese police service by integrating the present population's democratic demands; fostering a basic sense of accountability; and, finally, encouraging robust internal and external systems to monitor the reform.

Chapter 1, "Police reform a must", sets the stage for the analysis by questioning the PdP guiding principles, and scrutinising internal and external reformer expectations.

Chapter 2 explores the "winds of change," with a particular focus on the new legal framework on the implementation of reform. Issues like police recruitment, territorial deployment and police living and working conditions are tackled so as to highlight the complexity of a process that implies various internal and external dynamics.

Chapter 3 focuses on the crucial issue of reform resources and their distinctive characteristics. The chapter points to the lack of proper assessment of Congolese government budget realities and raises the fear that the present reform project may result in unrealistic expectations and unmanageable financial burdens.

Chapter 4, "Main police reform partners", provides a reading of the complex collaboration between internal and external reform partners, with a parti-

---

5   Insightful studies by Congolese scholars on security issues are increasingly available. See bibliography.

cular focus on the roles of the different partners and their hidden agendas that undermine the overall aims.

Chapter 5, "Contemplating roles of civil society", explores the conditions that promote a civil-police relationship, and examines partners who exchange, who do not take without giving.

Chapter 6, "Measuring effects", draws attention to the limited systematic measures of and reports on the impacts and indicators of progress in police reform. The study insists on the need to develop evaluation tools that measure outputs and outcomes of police reform in a comprehensive and informative way.

Chapter 7, "To conclude: What next?" recaps the main points of the study, listing a number of unanswered questions that will, it is hoped, alert internal and external reformers to the need to avoid repeating the constant cycle of failed reforms over and over and over again.

I.1. PdP reform: guiding principles

According to reformers, the Pdp concept is an answer to the urgent need to endow DRC with a democratic, republican, effective, civil, apolitical and professional police service. The PdP concept is based on six key principles, called the three **"Ps"** and the three **"Rs"** of community policing: **P**roximity, accessibility and availability of public services; **P**artnership and consultation; **P**revention and victim support; **R**esolving problems; **R**edevabilite (accountability) and transparency; and **R**espect for human rights

> At the heart of the Congolese proximity policing is the restoration of a confident relationship between the police and the population based on personalized and a-political police presence in the quarters. A proximity police is considered to be accessible to all and free of charge. Moreover, enshrined in the concept of proximity policing is the participative role of the population, through its civil society networks. Its implementation clearly requires a multidimensional policy approach. It does not solely focus on police structures, equipment and capacities. Perhaps even more important is the development of a chain of payment systems in order to guarantee free access to the police and reduce corruption, as well as the process of confidence-building between the police officers and the Congolese population.[6]

Obviously what internal and external reformers are courageously outlining is the shape of a people's police force that ceases to be an instrument of social

---

6 GMRRR Final Report. May 2006 www.reformedelapnc.org/documents/ GMRRRReport-en-Francais 2006.pdf. www.reformedelapnc.org.

control and refuses to legitimate present and future unpopular authoritarian regimes.

Below, we raise questions on reform strategies and tactics to integrate the above local and international dynamic and many others and avoid the constant cycle of failed reform in the history of the police in DRC. How local and international dynamics influence the reform process will emerge from the analysis in the section below that focuses on practical issues of the implementation of reform.

I.2. "Police de Proximité " or "Community policing"?

Central to reform is a clear statement of the concept or, better yet, of the new metaphor being introduced. Indeed, do the French *Police de Proximité* (PdP) concept and the British Community Policing simply produce the same style of policing? Don't they come from different traditions, namely the French civil law system and the British common law system? Obviously specialists involved in reform (Francophone and Anglophone) have different experiences of policing, although in the field they seem to work with the same model named "Police de Proximité" in documents in French and "Community Policing" in documents in English![7]

Further, as most Congolese officers hail from Francophone countries (former Belgian colony), we need to establish which area of policing they have in common with British community policing or Police de Proximité. And the challenge for Congolese reformers will be the development of a model relevant and appropriate to the Congolese context.

This last point is a call for collaboration between state and non-state actors in policing the urban and rural milieus. If the purpose is to improve police performance, can we not imagine a mechanism that delegates police powers to non-state actors in specific limited matters and stages of police surveillance operations, for instance?

---

7   "Both the common law system that prevailed in Commonwealth countries and the civil law in France, have produced a different style of policing. Common law systems trace their history to England, while civil law systems trace their history to Roman law and the French Napoleonic code. Common law systems place great weight on court decisions, which are considered 'law' with the same force of law as statutes. Common law courts have the authority to make law where no legislative statute exists, and statutes mean what courts interpret them to mean. By contrast, in civil law jurisdictions, courts lack authority to act where there is no statute, and judicial precedent is given less interpretive." Albrecht (2010) , p.31.

A comparative study of both systems yields the following insights.

Community police	Police de proximité
Implies the improvement of relations between the police and local communities	Implies the involvement [?] of institutional actors in the production of national, provincial and local strategic security plans. Framed by the national security system.
Limits itself to the image of the police at the local level. Therefore it is operative within limited territorial perimeters, often limited to the jurisdiction of the general commissioner. Administrative anchor is at the lowest level of the decentralised state and police organisation.	The range is wider because it is national, provincial and local. Administrative anchor is generally the commune or municipality.
Derives from the doctrine of the police de proximité aiming at improvement of community-police relations.	Closely linked to the issue of administrative decentralisation, urban policy and the need for consultation between institutional actors.

Indeed, shouldn't consolidation of the ongoing reform process also rely on local police initiatives and integrate them into a comprehensive national strategy whereby the state and communities support each other in a regulatory and normative framework defined at the national level?

Does ongoing police reform need to dismantle local community devices that provide "informal" policing, thereby obviously risking the creation of a security vacuum the state may not be able to fill?[8]

The above questions and others constantly emerge from the debates among or between providers and recipients of reform. They definitely call for a common understanding of the process's principles and goals. They suggest joint action between state and non-state actors preoccupied with promoting a new police service with an efficient and realistic policing philosophy and praxis.

Finally, these questions raise the issue of ownership of the PdP philosophy and project. CSRP and its executive secretariat, ordinary policemen/women and officers and the Congolese population have a shared responsibility for developing and elaborating reform policy and implementation.

The lack of a common implementation and training concept raises the spectre of the divergent implementation and functioning of proximity police in the country. With regard to national strategies, CSRP (an intra-Congolese coordination body involving various ministries) and external reform providers

---

8   On grassroots non-state organisations in the police sector, see: African Movement of Grassroots non-State Organizations (2009); RCN Justice et Démocratie (2010).

should obviously integrate lower levels in the Congolese police and society into their work to secure local partners' ownership and avoid creating strategies only valid at the national level, but not reflecting local expectations.

Ultimately, police reform has to be a bottom-up, civil society-oriented process, rather than one that is only elite-driven and oriented.

I.3. reform problems to overcome

The above six key principles summarise the problems to be resolved by both internal and external reformers. If they both seem to agree on these goals, the obvious problem to overcome is the gaps between the reform expectations of the providers and the recipients.

My research shows that these expectations are sometimes rather different. While Congolese rulers and police officers and other elements tend to think that the problem to solve is lack of good living and working conditions, lack of skills and equipment, lack of a good salaries, etc., external providers consider these issues as "symptomatic of a larger, systemic issues involving budgetary issues, mismanagement, leadership, planning, governance and so on".[9]

I.4. Donors' vs. Congolese police expectations

Donors' expectations	Congolese Police Officers' expectations
Community police: not a new unit but a new way of doing things and submitting to the needs of populations using a collaborative problem-solving approach	Community Police: a new unit, will be created from scratch
Insists on the government's will to improve police working conditions; to facilitate and promote police interaction with other security and administration services and finally to improve police relations with populations in a bid to secure some legitimacy for the new police	Welcomed the reform as it is synonymous with improved socio-professional conditions: reviewed salaries, new information and communication resources, new uniforms, new offices, decent housing units and improved healthcare, etc.

It is urgent to put an end to the above confusion because it has an impact on the tactics to be used to meet these different expectations. For instance, donors have tended to opt for well-financed sensitisation and other activities to ensure

---

9   It is worth mentioning the existence of police officers who also realize that the problem is one of mismanagement. They often do express informal criticisms of the government. Some of them are members of CSRP and others act at the provincial level.

the new philosophy is understood and implemented in certain pilot sites in Matadi (Bas-Congo), Kananga (Kasaï-Occidental) and Bukavu (Sud-Kivu).

The question raised by this tactic is "how to appease police officers from non-selected areas who see colleagues in a new and better equipped office and who simply, because they belong to an experimental pilot site, enjoy better conditions within the same police service?" Indeed, to what extent can such an operating style promote coherence within the national police? Doesn't it have the opposite effect by creating competition and distrust rather than collaboration among colleagues? Certainly, the project has to start somewhere. But my fear is that this approach will create disorder rather than serve as a means to gradually diffuse excellence throughout the police.

Three problems are associated with meeting police officers' expectations.

First, both the government's commitment to policing and its capacity to fund policing activities are often called into question. If donors are inclined to support improvements to work infrastructure and equipment, they can only finance these changes for a specific period. It is up to the national government to provide the resources to allow the police to accomplish their tasks appropriately.

Second, it is important that substantial change occur to improve the image of the police. But it is also important to sustain the improvements so that the progress made will not be erased by ever-decreasing sources of funding, a phenomenon familiar in most reforms in the South that rely on external funding.[10]

Obviously, the underlying issues are sustainability, cohesion and relevance to avoid repetition of past reforms that very often failed once external support came to an end.

Third, if police officers and agents think the problem is inadequate salaries, skills and equipment, they must realise that these problems are symptomatic of larger systemic issues, including budgetary issues, (mis)management, leadership, planning, governance, among many others.

As highlighted in many interviews, there is a need for a holistic approach that addresses the establishment of a police force based on a statute that clarifies the responsibilities of civilians, police authorities and other security services and is rooted in a solid career management plan promoting access to better living and working conditions.

---

10 For instance, the "Garde civile" experiment in Mobutu's time. The project failed soon after German financial support ended. Also, the short PdP experiment in Nzanza commune, Bas-Congo, October 2013. Moreover, police reform in Sierra Leone experienced serious problems at the end of the British funding period.

II. The winds of change

Can we assume that donor funding was the major factor that ensured that police reform became a priority after the 2006 elections? Was it the return to multiparty democracy? Was it the governmental priority of restoring law and order? Was it the challenge to restore a friendly image to the police to ensure good community relations? Or was it the population that was longing for local policing that guaranteed the safety and security of all people and their property?

It is obvious that the winds of change result from a combination of factors, but in which order: external donors-Congolese government-police and population or Congolese population-police-government and external donors?

Answers to these questions are important and need to be clear. Indeed they shed light on the level of appropriation and sustainability of the reform project. The first combination explains the passivity of members of the police force and probably why few initiatives come from their side. In this first combination, the police force is the receiver of a new metaphor, a new philosophy, of funds, infrastructure, equipment, training, etc.

The second combination is initiated by those who are most affected by the reforms, namely Congolese police officers, and the external partners are there in support. National ownership and sustainability of the project can be better achieved through the second process. In this scenario, the police force can be more proactive and creative actors.

These Congolese police reformers[11] are aware that the promotion of a community police force is inextricably linked to improved salaries and social conditions, and would require an audit of police numbers. This courageous act would end the use of fictitious employees whose salaries help senior officers supplement their own pay.[12]

II.1. 2011: another police legal establishment

After the legal evolution that led to the creation of the National Congolese Police in 2002, it took nine years or more to ratify and promulgate the organic law defining the mission and organisation of the new police.

---

11 These internal police reformers organised the Comité pour le Suivi de la Réforme de la Police (CSRP).

12 Various actors are involved in this operation: CSRP, RRSSJ, and EUSEC. Recently, the government has initiated a police payment procedure through the banks in the hopes of obtaining an accurate tally of the number of police officers.

The final document that emerged in 2011 proposes to separate the police force into an administrative branch (*police administrative*) and a legal branch (*police judiciaire*), both of which are to work with the judiciary to prosecute offences. It also establishes five police structures, namely the Superior Council, General Commissionership, Inspectorate General, provincial police stations and territorial and local units.

However, the final document was a watered-down version of the initial proposal and is considered by some to be a step backward. The law as it stands does not include consensual decisions made by civil society and political leaders. For instance:[13]

- The initial proposal included the concept of police cohesion, but the senate's select committee chose to merge some branches of the police, instead of integrating them. This applies to the *Police des parquets* (Police Force in charge of prosecutions), the administrative arm of the police, the ANR and the DGM. The new law does not grant administrative or financial autonomy to the PNC.
- Issues of gender-based violence and child protection, the Framework Act on PNC reform and the structural composition of the police service have also been left out by senators
- The initial bill on the organisation and structure of the police included three bodies: the *Conseil supérieur de la police* (superior police council) was to be a consultative body; the *Commissariat général* (general commissionership), was meant as a commanding and operational structure; the *Inspection générale* (general inspectorate) was to be the supervisory body. Interestingly, the new document establishes provincial police commissioners or police stations as autonomous structures operating alongside the *Commissariat général*. The same goes for the *Direction générale des ecoles et des formations* (Schools and Training General Directorate), which is an integral part of the *Commissariat sénéral*.

The most likely scenario is that these issues will continue to be debated while the reform is being implemented. It will be interesting to see how the new police service will operate without the integration of the *Police judiciaire des parquets* and the *Police des frontiers* (border police) within it, and how it will resolve the duplication of units and specialists, which is partly responsible for its current problems.

---

13 Nlandu Mayamba (2012c), pp. 51, 53.

With regard to the financial and administrative autonomy of the police, experts agree there is an inherent contradiction between the very nature of the police as a public service, and the refusal to treat the force as such by granting it the autonomy it requires. One can also question how the police will address important issues such as gender-based violence, child protection and promoting hygiene and salubriousness, all of which have been left out of the current law, but are central to the police's public service mission?

Although reformers officially welcomed the promulgation of the organic law as a significant development in PNC reform, one should mention that parliamentary validation of the documents took two years. Indeed the triennial plan and the idea of proximity policing were validated in 2008-09. The organic law was, however, passed in 2011!

The above processes and problems clearly indicate the need to improve relationships between key Congolese actors in charge of the reform process. Although this does not seem possible, it is urgent to seek actual support from the higher echelons of power to avoid undermining the sustainability of the efforts and frightening off European partners and others from engaging in the long run. More pressure should be put on parliament both by Congolese civil society and external partners to act as a counterweight and cease protecting the interests of the executive and the majority of parliamentarians by simply rubber-stamping decisions.

The majority in parliament should stop pressing on with reforms that have been prioritised by the president, and delaying those thought to be a potential threat to the government's operations (police, army and security service, justice and decentralisation reforms).

II.2. Implementation calendar

The police reform journey started in 2002 during the Inter-Congolese Dialogue. In 2005, the then minister for home affairs and security initiated the Mixed Reflection Group on the Reform and the Reorganisation of the Congolese National Police (GMRRR or GMR³). In 2006-07, GMR³ presented its conclusions and recommendations, including a draft proposal for an organic law on the functioning and organisation of the CNP. In 2007, based on the GMR³ recommendations, a Police Reform Follow-up Committee (*Comité de Suivi de la Réforme de la Police*) was created by the minister for the interior and security.

The CSRP produced significant conceptual work on reform. Most importantly, it elaborated a long-term (15 year) strategic framework and a short-term (triennial) action plan for police reform. Both plans were validated in the working year 2008–09 and adopted by the Congolese government in 2010. As noted above, it is only more recently, in 2011, that the organic law organising the police and defining its mission was promulgated, nine years after the 2002 decision to initiate the reform.

These and other delays raise many troubling questions about the extremely volatile personal relations between key actors in the CSRP; about CSRP's formal decision-making competence, efficiency and credibility; about the extremely centralised decision-making power in formal and informal networks surrounding President Kabila; and finally about the willingness of internal and external reform providers to engage in a long-term process whose validity risks being questioned and whose sustainability risks being undermined.[14]

II.3. Recruitment and territorial deployment

To "respond to citizens' needs for peace and tranquillity", the territorial organisation of the new police requires revision to align police structures with political and administrative subdivisions involving 26 provinces, instead of the formal 11.[15]

While politicians seek to create new small provinces, the question remains as to how the police recruitment plans and geographic deployment can be designed in such a way as to cement national unity?

The answer is probably a recruitment policy that takes the diversity of the population into account (ratio, activity and sensitivity); that strengthens national unity by no longer recruiting deserters, looters and offenders; and that refuses to build the police using former rebels.[16]

There is no need to bury one's head in the sand like an ostrich. The integration mechanism, metaphorically called brassage and "mixage",[17] has shown its weaknesses and damaging effects by destabilising the army, the police and the whole security sector in terms of cohesion, morale and performance.

---

14 Justaert (2011), pp. 13–17.
15 Congolese Constitution (18 February 2006) and Organic Law no 08/016 (7 October 2008).
16 Such a practice was witnessed in the 1960s with the integration of former Gendarmes Katangais. Later, after the Mulele rebellion, former Mulelists were integrated into the police. Recently, since the MLC and RCD agreement, this recruitment mechanism is still in use, with police recruits labelled "Les intégrés".
17 Yamba Tshintu (2012). In South and North Kivu, soldiers integrated into the police are called "Les intégrés".

Restoring honour, dignity and pride to the police profession starts with a courageous decision to cease considering this service as a dumping ground for undisciplined men and women from different communities, and offenders and opportunists of any kind. The police as an institution cannot transform a piece of wood into a crocodile.[18]

Now that the nation is forming a national police force, suggestions for autonomous local security spheres of influence, and for police elements and officers who serve at a local or provincial level should be strongly questioned. The problem with localised or territorial security provisions is that they risk strengthening local, regional and ethnic identity rather than a national one.[19] Such a solution cannot be acceptable, because it does not echo the PdP philosophy or principles and does not help police actors "to sing from the same hymn sheet".

Recruitment and geographic deployment must offer a legally recognised equal right of access to public positions for all Congolese, regardless of geographical origin. This implies respect for ethnic and regional balance in the composition of police units, but also a balancing of command and a basic respect for meritocracy.

The recruitment of candidates to the new police should require a basic qualification equivalent to a baccalaureate or secondary school state diploma. In addition, candidates should have one or two year's civic service.

Consequently, no homogeneous units should be integrated into the police as an operating entity with all its components intact. All identifiable homogeneous units operating now as police in a given province must be dismantled and their members reassigned to various units throughout the country. This is the case with the police units in Katanga, where the majority of police agents belong to that province. The same situation is evident in North Kivu, where police agents of the M23 rebel movement are essentially members of the same ethnic group. All provinces must be equally represented at all levels in the making of the new national police. No ethnic group should receive preferential treatment in terms of rank, police elements or officers in any particular province, nor can such group comprise the major component of the police, as is today the case in some parts of the country.

To ensure police operational effectiveness, recruitment policy should end the practice whereby each "chief" has "his" police elements, which are not

---

18 This strong statement was made by General Mahele during the 1992 Congolese National Sovereign Conference, Kinshasa.
19 Nlandu Mayamba (2012a).

truly integrated into a coherent police force (General Numbi controls "his" men, General Amisi "his" men, Sultani Makenga, and many others, each having "his" own PdP or soldiers, etc.). The variability of Congolese PdPs has been a longstanding menace to the people and even to the government they are supposed to protect.[20] Like the army in DRC, the police have become an internal threat.

The goal of this new recruitment policy based on sufficient training, plurality and meritocracy is to avoid the practice, on the pretext of "peace before justice" or "the nation is one and indivisible", among policy makers to recruit only within their ethnic circle, to the detriment of other ethnic groups and regions of the country. Such a recruitment policy has produced disappointing results in the past and should not to be repeated.

II.4. Police personnel rejuvenation

This operation involves both the implementation of a stepping-down or retirement plan for policemen and women who have reached the professional age limit, and the recruitment of new elements to ensure succession.

In the short term, the decision will affect all police personnel who have reached or passed 60 years. How many of them are there among the approximately 103,808[21] police elements. This is unknown, due to the lack of formal accounting mechanism.

The latest known figures suggest that less than 96,614 of the 103,808 police are active. With proper controls, the estimated reduction in numbers might be 40 per cent, leaving the police force with less than 60,000 active personnel.

These data are important, because they determine the optimum recruitment level, the ideal ratio being one policeman to 360 inhabitants.[22] This ratio would suggest a police body of 166,000 elements in coming years. To achieve this goal, 10,000 men and women need to be recruited per year over 10 years, a considerable undertaking and difficult to envisage, given the reality of state means.[23]

---

20 The structure of such a police, characterised by variability of police units, will not permit different units to be integrated into a coherent police force with an effective command structure.

21 GMRRR PNC (2007), p. 23.

22 Ibid., p.37.

23 Ibid.

Nevertheless, taking into account the complexity of the personnel rejuvenation operation, the present study can simply suggest some conditions under which it could be organised. Police personnel with a brilliant past career who leave must be helped in returning to and reintegrating into civil life, and ways must be found to harness their skills. For example, retired general Inspectors and officers could start new lives in central government or territorial administrations as advisers on police and security matters.

The state must find other rewarding social readjustment mechanisms in support of other categories. Creating a solidarity fund to assist retired policemen and women might be an answer: the state and private institutions could provide subsidies to the fund.

II.5. equipment acquisition and Training

If the reform aims at creating a professional, modern and credible force, the Congolese police must be well trained and led by a dedicated staff. They must have sufficient equipment in terms of quantity and quality; a relevant budget; sufficient finance; and good doctrine and deontology. The police force ought to be effective, credible and respected, with a reliable leadership and stable structures.

The modernity of the Congolese police will be attested by its doctrines, appropriate technology, dynamic well-trained leadership, efficient communication systems; its ability to respond to any kind of disaster; the flexibility of its structures and its logistical independence.

From the above, it follows that the reopening of police training and instruction schools, centres for the training of recruited elements, is an urgent recommendation. This requires the rehabilitation of existing infrastructure (Kasapa, Kapalata, Jules Moke, Hewa Bora, MvulaMatadi, and Kasangulu), the acquisition of training materials and equipment, the training of trainers and the harmonisation of programmes.

The reformed training system must insist on the use of a doctrine for training and tactics adapted to Congolese realities. It must acquire equipment and police material that can be easily maintained and replaced. And finally, it should lobby for an overall command structure for police schools under the direction of Inspectorate staff, to avoid the direct dependency of police schools on the ministry of the interior.

As far as the training programme is concerned, the curriculum must highlight the specific issues faced by police and train personnel in values, ethics and professional ethos. Human rights issues, police and gender, police and sexual violence and finally police and vulnerable groups should be at the heart of the police training programme in the DRC.

The main idea is to convert the police into a service respectful of human rights; which puts man and woman at the heart of its action; which recognises the rights of every human being irrespective of his or her race, religion, nationality, political or ideological convictions. These rights are guaranteed by national and international legal instruments and are intended to ensure the development of the human being.

The police must be informed of the corrective measures in the constitutional provisions and the organic law, and control mechanisms such as the IGA, in order to really put the human being at the centre of an officer's actions.

As a public service, the police must ensure strict observance of gender equality. This should be clearly evident in recruitment, orientation, promotion and functions. In fulfilling its mission, the police force is also called upon to engage resolutely in the fight against sexual violence.

In their activities, the police are urged to take into account gender specificities. Thus, a woman should not be in the same cell as men in order to reduce the risk of sexual violence. Women should also be given the chance to discharge the same functions and enjoy the same responsibilities as men.

The successive wars in DRC; the presence of various foreign and domestic armed groups, militias and police agents; the illicit circulation of war weapons; and the impoverishment of the population have meant that sexual violence has become a scourge experienced on a daily basis. Women and girls are particularly vulnerable, and armies and police, particularly in eastern Congo, are among the primary perpetrators of murder, rape, torture, and extortion.[24]

Considering the extent of sexual violence in the DRC, the police are called upon to improve the system of preventing and suppressing such offences and of ensuring its members refrain from conduct that promotes the commission of these crimes.

Vulnerable groups, for instance, children, disadvantaged women, people living with mental or physical disabilities and the elderly, need special protection and guidance for their well-being.

To conclude, the new police must be aware of the links between police action and the specific issues which arise within a community and require police and community attention. The ability to recognise such issues will be aided thanks to the police force's ability to address identity-based tensions and

---

24 Compelling insights on sexual violence in wartime can be found in Eriksson Baaz and Stern (2013).

discrimination in promotions and distribution of functions and command positions within its own ranks.

One observation from my research is that well-trained police elements and officers from certain ethnic groups (from Equateur particularly and the western and central parts of the country) are often neglected. They play secondary roles and "feel systematically disadvantaged in the distribution of position and functions, and subjected to unjust and unfair treatment in relation to informal and formal punitive actions and disciplining".[25]

As highlighted above, the police must comply with the law and behave responsibly in all circumstances to become true guardians of the population. To reach this objective, mechanisms or approaches to cooperation must be developed between police and populace.

II.6. Improving living and working conditions

The policeman, like every citizen, enjoys all the fundamental rights afforded human beings and guaranteed by the constitution, except for those express restrictions prescribed by law.[26] Like any citizen, the police officer is also subject to duties and other obligations. Reformers must always keep in mind that civilians who have chosen to serve in the police ultimately want employment and opportunities, and not to beg or steal from the population in order to survive.

Police reform ought to place the policeman and woman at the centre of its concerns by improving their social and professional conditions. Concretely, the reform should increase salaries and social services, such as medical care and funeral expenses.[27]

It is urgent to establish a relevant minimum salary for every last policeman and woman. The parliamentary commission in charge of security sector reforms should be able to give an overall estimate of these costs. Indeed, this institution can give some thought as to what is affordable.

---

25 Following Maria Eriksson Baaz and interviewed police officers, we confirm the above feelings, all factors that undermine morale, cohesion and command structure in the police and army. See Eriksson Baaz, pp.27-9.

26 For example: prohibition to vote, to get involved in commercial activities and politics.

27 Salaries range from 62,000. Franc Congolais (900 FC= 1dol.) for a simple police constable to 90,000 FC for a full colonel in 2013. Data obtained from CSRP, RD Congo.

Better police living and working conditions call for the application of legal texts and statutes that codify the management of police careers. The new legal approach will determine the specificities of police public service. This bill is essential to reform, because it deals with living and working conditions for police, with particular attention to his family life. It is also concerned with the agent's life after he has faithfully served in the police.

The improvement of police well-being is a must if the reform efforts of both internal and external providers are not to be undermined. Experts expect that the state's effectiveness in ensuring police welfare, combined with its tackling issues such as patronage and Big-Man networks, will hopefully address present concerns about officers' involvement in politics and commercial activities that gives rise to predatory lawlessness and undermines social cohesion.

Indeed, once in power, nominally civilian former soldiers tend, thanks to facade of democratic elections, to encourage significant military involvement in business to reward former comrades in the liberation army. They enrich themselves through business so that together they can successfully control society via members of armed forces, militarised police and intelligence services.[28]

Given this situation, humanising police working and living conditions is probably a good strategy to keep police officers and others out of politics and the economy. This reform could end police officers' negative role in the economy and politics if it wisely accompanies the present wider transformation of police and army forces into "a group of citizens".[29]

Failure to improve living and working conditions of this group of citizens that held power for years will weaken the reform process and could trigger revolts and even plant the seeds of rebellion. The reform will have destabilising and disabling effects if it leaves the police actors in poverty, with little or no money for basics.

The ultimate success of police reform depends on continued support for the trained units, for even well trained and equipped units can disintegrate or turn against the local population if they are not regularly paid and kept under responsible administrative and political control.

The conclusions of the first Pdp test in Matadi are telling. Indeed, they confirm that for the police, reform should put more emphasis on logistical aspects rather than on those aspects related to the individual transformation

---

28 Doss, Herbst and Mills (2013), p.9.
29 Ibid., p.8.

of police officers. Hence effective national ownership of the reform is crucial to success in improving the living and working conditions of police officers.[30]

This time round, although meeting these challenges is clearly a huge task, if the police and many other related security sector reforms flop, the regime and the international community backing it can expect trouble.

---

30 Mayambula Nkoyi-Sweswe (2012), pp. 14–15.

III. Partners and resources in police reform

A number of development partners support the government in its efforts to construct and rehabilitate police infrastructure, and provide useful technical advice, equipment, vehicles, information, and staff training. The resources mobilised by international actors are of three kinds: normative, financial and advocacy.

III.1. Normative resources

International police reform providers in DRC do not agree on the same standards, even if they all refer to the OECD vision based on human security.[31] Indeed with regard to police reform, Anglo-Saxon actors, particularly the British (DFID) and UNDP, promote a vision of the police largely based on "community policing", which is not necessarily consistent with the community policing approach (PdP) promoted by the European Union through the EUPOL mission and adopted by the CSRP.

III.2. international financial resources

It is true that various international actors mobilise significant financial resources. Access to these data and particularly to the detailed breakdown of the budget is not always easy. Several analyses confirm that there are problems with the current financing provided.

- It is often volatile, circumstantial and not sustainable, and supports changes to the legal facade in place of real and lasting change that puts humans at the heart of the projects.[32]
- There is an imbalance in the distribution of funds, 70 per cent of which are for equipment and training and 30 per cent to improve the formulation of popular requests in the area of security and to better popular control of this sector.[33]

---

31 Most Western donors rely on the documents developed by the OECD Development Assistance Committee (DAC), the key forum in which bilateral donors, the EU, UNDP, IMF and the World Bank coordinate development cooperation policies. For its guidelines, see OECD (2004).
32 The best illustration is the promotion of facade democratic regimes following multiparty elections of radically varying quality.
33 According to interviewed police officers, only the taste for new equipment, which some external actors are happy to supply, usually at a price, can explain this disequilibrium.

In my view, this disequilibrium can be seen as one of the negative incentives for foreign involvement in security sector reform. In many regards, police reform in the DRC, like army and justice reforms, has become an industry. Precious little of the funding "hits the ground", that is, is left over after payment of the exorbitant bills for ill-adapted training and inappropriate equipment, which very often cannot be easily maintained or replaced.

III.3. National financial resources

The reforms need colossal financial resources in order to be successful. Yet, they must first rely on the internal national resources mobilised by the government. Input from external partners should be secondary in making the reforms sustainable. Unfortunately, so far the financial burden is carried by international partners, with a weak contribution by government.

This raises the question of how the reforms will fare once donor funding runs out or when the project comes to its end. What are the available internal means of raising revenue in a context undermined by corruption and impunity?

At the national level, it is an illusion and even dangerous to think the Congolese government will achieve financial self-dependence in four or five years to manage the present complex police reforms put in place by external donors.

Personally, I worry about the lack of proper assessment of Congolese government budget realities, the absence of a realistic long-term financial support plan and of a clear, negotiated donor exit strategy or even of a withdrawal plan based on mutual consent. On paper, the reforms seem like a good idea, but I am afraid that in financial terms they remain less successful as a practical proposal. My perception is that the present reform project is building unrealistic expectations and unmanageable financial burdens.

III.4. Lobbying resources

Very often neglected in debates is the issue of the capacity of international donors to mobilise lobbying resources to build the necessary political will among national policy-makers to promote reforms in the security sector.

Indeed, anxious not to interfere, but, at the same time, increasingly concerned about results, international networks are more and more forced to act beyond the simple mobilisation of finance and expertise. Donors can impose various reforms as the price of assistance. They can act in collaboration with internal reformers in the commissions in parliament and in the police system. In collaboration with empowered civil society structures, they can lobby the parliament and the government.

IV. Main police reform partners

Usually, the debate on the reformers tends to focus on political and administrative actors, both internal and external, who provide support to reform. Very little is said about the profile of the Congolese police officers involved in the reform.

Tactically, I would recommend the recruitment of senior police officers with a serious university background, whose aspiration is to be part of a policing body that brings changes and reforms to the Congolese police. These are the senior officers who should be on board the restructuring train, with a general inspector at their head, a national or international figure with no political affiliations or attachments.[34]

What the reform needs at this level is someone who would actually be able to make difficult decisions to bring change; someone able to identify reform-minded police officers and to encourage or retire people who do not share the vision of the reform. We must keep in mind that actors willing to reform do exist in many layers of the Congolese police. These probably are the ones who offer their expertise to the CSRP.

Obviously, the debate is still open about who, Congolese or foreigner, could be appointed to head up the reformers efficiently? Although the tendency would be to appoint a foreigner, the issue is how to ensure that this appointment does not appear to be political or neo-colonial?[35]

IV.I. international reform partners

Several international partners are involved: European Union (EUPOL mission), UN (MONUSCO police division and UNDP) and DFID (SSAPR project), France, Belgium, Angola and South Africa.

---

34 Such a debate took place in Mobutu's time when Mr. Blumenthal, a German, was appointed governor of the Central Bank, and Mr. Pawlinks, a Belgian, general director of ONATRA.

35 As in Sierra Leone, the appointment of a foreigner would probably have the support of honest Congolese police officers and the bulk of ordinary Congolese. Indeed, corruption and impunity in DR Congo have reached such proportions that many Congolese confess they were better off under Belgian colonial rule! It is sad but true that most Congolese would rather be led by foreigners than by their own failed political class! See Doyle (1999).

The police cooperation is heteroclite and dispersed among several and even competing donors with varying standards and approaches to doctrine and deployment. This kaleidoscope[36] of actors operates in a decentralised and scattered way.

This reality is attested by various postcolonial police reform projects. It also confirms why no articulated, viable and appropriate police reform emerged from most of these projects, which provoked great resentment among the police and populace because of their lack of coordination.[37]

Indeed, how could a sense of national identity possibly be strengthened among the police with all these competing partners each training a police unit in a specific corner of the country? What efficient joint operations could be expected from these disparate units with diverging philosophies, very often rooted in mutual distrust?

One example of divergent traditions and philosophies can be found in the different approaches to crowd policing among partners such as Angola and the EU. It seems that in managing the street protests before and after the 2006 and 2011 elections, most police performed quite well, with the exception of the Angolan-trained units, which adopted a heavy-handed approach to crowd control.[38] How could todays' victims of repression distinguish between two forces wearing the same Congolese police uniforms?

IV.2. International partners trapped by reforms

The enthusiasm for reform expressed in various legal texts and praxis since independence in DR Congo raises intriguing questions that deserve attention. Indeed, what explains external and internal reformers' enthusiasm during these years of failed police reforms? Does the reason for failure only lie in the Congolese political decision-makers' lack of political will? What are the consequences of bilateral donors' police assistance strategies that are not rooted in clear joint strategic planning? Why have external partner training

---

36 The strategic location of DRC, together with the diversity of the country's economic resources, probably explains the nature of this cooperation.

37 EU, Angola and Japanese assistance programmes, to name but a few, obviously involve competing donors with varying standards and approaches to doctrine and deployment.

38 Angola provides military training to the police, an approach that does not hesitate to use lethal weapons for crowd control.

programmes always focused on police crowd control, while neglecting basic investigation techniques?

Answering these questions will allow for better understanding of the internal and external dynamics governing the police reform process in DRC. The success of police reform requires that both internal and external reformers acknowledge the dynamics that undermine their common official goals.

Insofar as Congolese rulers are concerned, present and past reforms have simply been opportunities to acquire new tools for social control and for regime protection. Fragile and weak leaders of a disjointed nation are ready to accept what the donors wish to or can provide, given that it improves police efficiency in crowd control. In this context, they can even accept project-by-project assistance that lacks a coherent strategy or articulated terms of disengagement.

Then, the main embarrassing question has always been how to sell such deficient projects to democratic Western governments facing financial scarcity and ever more accountable to their own electorates regarding international policy?

Thanks to a subtle approach that does not determine which act precedes the other, reform and assistance demands come together to promote cooperation that external providers of police reform in DRC can easily explain to their national tax contributors.

The step that follows confirms local partners' "ownership" of the police reform project. This probably explains the rapid creation of weak and inefficient structures such as the CSRP, the Civil Society Network for the Reform of the Security and Justice Sectors[39] and a financially unsustainable PdP concept, given present DRC authorities' handling of budget issues.

---

39 Nlandu Mayamba (2006), pp.44–55. Ideas developed in this paper can also explain the RRSSJ network weaknesses:

* First, the network permanently faces serious survival tests due to the absence of a robust succession plan mainly when its leadership get absorbed into CSRP, international organisations (MONUSCO, EUPOL, SSAPR, DAI, etc.), parliament and government;

* Second, the donors' decision to support and legitimate the established nominally democratic government resulted in a dramatic drying up of funds for a network, which, like many civil society organisations, relies on an essentially donor-generated budget;

* Third, the so-called democratic age necessitates a very delicate balancing act, and imposes a new network mode of engagement, including collaboration without becoming "collabos".

Consequently, as in many reform initiatives, enthusiastic internal and external reformers are ensnared, with, unfortunately, the Congolese population, supposedly the main beneficiaries of reform, continuing to face an uncertain future

Congolese decision-makers consider the reform process to be a good opportunity for acquiring a well-equipped and trained police unit to tame, repress and punish civilians. This approach is all too reminiscent of both the colonial and Mobutu eras, specifically the former *Force Publique* and *Garde-Civile*,[40] a kind of anti-riot police force modelled on the German federal police and financed by Germany.

This body was well equipped with specialist equipment such as truck-mounted water cannons, teargas and lethal weapons. It included anti-terrorist, canine and marine units. And although this was not the intent behind German cooperation, this unit soon became the regime's favourite elite unit.

More recently, in answer to "electoral requirements", international partners provided training and equipment focused on crowd control in a move reminiscent of the colonial and Mobutu eras.[41]

Many of the Congolese government and external reformers interviewed officially or unofficially confirm that since independence they have shared the same agenda with the ruling class, namely to ensure the stability of successive predatory regimes for the benefit of warlords and other "big men and women",[42] who for decades pillaged the country's resources together with international and regional predators.

"Elections" today, like the restoration of "public order" in the past, offer the opportunity to support the less sure-footed Congolese leaders that emerged through messy compromises.

This explains why before, during and after elections, the newly trained police units stand as a robust presence ready not to protect Congolese civilians, but to step in at short notice to protect a vulnerable regime that emerged from an unfair electoral process and thus lacks legitimacy[43] It is not surprising, therefore, that the efficiency of these new police is evaluated on the basis of

---

40 Nlandu Mayamba (2012c), p. 25.
41 Obviously, the insidious thing is that although the aim of the training has always been the protection of the population, the trained units become the favourite elite force for protecting the regime.
42 Utas (2012), pp. 1–31.
43 DR Congo had multiparty elections in 2006 and 2011. In spite of the urge to democratise across the country, Congolese people are generally disappointed with the authoritarian anti-democratic regime that has evolved since.

their ability to handle rallies seeking the truth of the ballot, and in terms of the level of violence they commit in doing so.

International partners dedicated to the reform must understand these local, regional and international dynamics if they do not want to undermine their goals and erode the legitimacy of their actions. From the outset, they must constantly make it clear in theory and praxis that PdP is not and will not be a newly created intervention unit enjoying preferential treatment, either in its development or in its staffing.

Success in addressing the above issues and others that will occur in the reform process is dependent on sustained and enhanced communication between external and internal reformers.

In conclusion, in this "hide and seek game", or to use the "positive Chinese metaphor" in vogue in Africa, this "win-win" police reform cooperation, all external partners make profits that confirm macroeconomic growth for the minority but guarantee macro-poverty to the majority at the periphery of global welfare. Indeed, both Western governments preoccupied with the promotion of human rights and the maintenance of a facade democracy in DRC and the Chinese, interested in business rather than in human rights or democracy, act and operate according to their interests.

Indeed:

> In many countries, for example, natural resource revenues are widening the gap between rich and poor. Although much has been achieved, a decade of highly impressive growth has not brought comparable improvements in health, education and nutrition. [44]

IV.3. what reform expects from government

The police reform process in DRC needs a democratic space that will confirm the government's commitment to the reforms. The reform requires an enabling environment to ensure its successful and sustainable implementation. In addition to the elaboration and promulgation of the law, the government needs to concretely establish the primacy of the police as providers of internal security in DRC. This can be achieved through governmental action that integrates the following four key elements: rule of law, accountability, transparency, accessibility and affordability.

Above all, leadership mentoring, and especially training in local budgetary, procurement and logistics processes, is lacking. Consequently, the will of

---

44 Read: Africa Progress Panel. (2013), foreword by Kofi Annan.

34

Congolese political leaders in power to promote police reform is not reinforced. Indeed, police reform demands that DRC takes a lead, notably by setting aside sufficient and constant budgeted funds.

Training police men and women in various camps throughout the country using the best external police expertise and equipping them with the most sophisticated equipment is not the main problem. Rather, it is the system that supports police elements and officers, namely the civil institutions in which police elements are located or those the police have to work with, that are deficient and undermine the prospects of the DRC police reform process.[45]

Furthermore, successful police reform would have to audit police numbers. This would end the use of fictitious employees to supplement senior officers' pay.

The police reform plan proposed no eradication of impunity, a main source of indiscipline in the national force. The reform plan is also silent on the nature and quality of civil-police relations. And yet such relationships are a key criterion for evaluating policing in any democratic state.

Definitely, the main challenge for government remains the establishment and implementation of the principle of democratic control of the police and security sector through good governance, especially oversight, accountability and transparency. This will require a move away from a police force in which professional progress depends on connections rather than qualifications and expertise.

That is why I personally fear that the announced presidential intention to endow DRC with "a National Police, a republican, elitist and legalistic force … to both establish democracy and serve Congolese people"[46] simply adds to the list of unfulfilled promises. And my fears are justified.

First, a firm understanding of the personality and motives of President Kabila and various networks in power is central to any reform strategy.

Second, the reform is led by former soldiers who came to power via AFDL, a "liberation" army movement. The now nominal civilians have a very low opinion of civilian supremacy or of promoting accountable political control or even reform that might weaken their grip on power.[47]

---

45 Obasanjo et al. (2013). General Obasanjo's assumption also applies to the police in DR Congo!

46 Kabila (2011).

47 Examples of armies that have morphed into civilian regimes include Angola, Burkina Faso Chad, DR Congo, Congo-Brazzaville, Rwanda, Uganda, Gambia, Namibia, Eritrea anc Ethiopia, to name but a few.

Third, the present government that emerged from a messy electoral process is vulnerable. Weakness or failure to carry out vital reforms can in part be explained by the military's "civilianised" leaders' and elite failures to police themselves. They have limited moral weight, no real legitimacy within Congolese society and institutions such as the police and army. They have broken down the internal mechanisms that usually create legitimate centres of power. There is a limited ethnic, political, military and economic base from which they derive legitimacy and to which they are accountable.

Hence, to survive, the nominally civilian Congolese rulers and elite insidiously and constantly engage with civil society in economic and political activities that undermine any reform that might question the presence of numerous formal and informal actors in the strategic spheres of political and economic power. These rulers are frequently named as participants in various illegal commercial activities.[48]

Fourth, the police reforms launched with the promulgation of the 2011 laws need other legal instruments that still languish in parliament or on the president's desk. Such is the case with the police statute, the law on the Superior Council of Defence and various laws on decentralisation, to name but a few.

Lastly, issues such as the audit of police numbers and vetting within the police still worry the Congolese populace. Further, this project raises questions about the present army recruitment campaign, even though the government has not yet finalised the audit of personnel or fixed staff retirement modalities.

IV.4. when impunity undermines justice reform

The restructuring of the Supreme Court is required for the effective promotion of the rule of law in DRC. The 2006 constitution splits the former Supreme Court into three separate jurisdictional orders (the Constitutional Court, the State Council and the Supreme Court of Judicature) and establishes new jurisdictions (work, commerce and administrative tribunals). The judicial arrangements include civil and military jurisdictions under the control of the Supreme Court. The Congolese judicial system is based on a Roman-Germanic model and the French and Belgian systems in particular.

Thirteen years after justice sector reform was initiated, no major progress can be noted. The report of UN Secretary-General Ban Ki-Moon on 30 March 2010 remains accurate.[49] Civil justice operates on less than 1 per cent of the

---

48 See Verweijen (2013), pp. 67–82.
49 UN Secretary General (30 March 2010), §44.

national budget. No administrative structure is in place to manage finances or personnel, ensure the monitoring of cases, prepare the budget and handle the assets. Cases of official interference in the administration of justice and corruption are frequently reported.

In cases of misconduct by policemen and women, sanctions are applied both at professional level (disciplinary actions by the hierarchy) and in court (penalties handed down by the military court).

Note that since October 2010 a General Inspection division exists that examines civilian complaints about police abuse, thereby showing that at least on paper police officers are no longer above the law.

However, even though Congolese rulers claim that the question of justice and impunity are a high priority, impunity for the most senior police remains a serious preoccupation for both national and international communities. The military High Court is powerless and cannot charge army or police chiefs (cf., John Numbi and Chebeya's case; Gabriel Amisi, Sabiti, etc.).

The Court shields its weakness behind the principle of "peace before justice", a principle that probably allows the circulation in total liberty of warlords and other criminals wanted by national and international justice systems. Security sector reform is made more complicated by the refusal to rid the sector of elements seriously suspected of massive human rights violations or implicated in the illegal exploitation of natural resources as well as the maintenance of armed groups. The police are thus prevented from getting rid of elements guilty of serious failures of military duty and discipline.

But this principle has brought neither peace nor justice. Hence the need for DRC justice officials to initiate proceedings against officers named in a UN experts' report for their role in maintaining armed groups, trafficking in weapons and illegally exploiting resources. It is important to demonstrate the DRC government's determination to combat impunity and end electoral fetishism that institutionalises the fallacy of statehood and creates a democratic facade that enables the failure of reform.

IV.5. Beyond facade democracy

In Congo, the world of citizens and the world of political decision-makers have moved apart. A whole range of signs indicate the disturbed nature of the relationship between citizens and politics, between the population and those who govern. Reinventing a new governance/government for a new police is a must.

The relationship has manifested separatist tendencies: people in power treating the Other as objects to be explored, exploited and controlled. With total arrogance, these so-called enlightened political leaders have cut the chord to the source of political legitimacy.

Congolese citizens are disappointed with facade democracy and its fake, fetish multiparty elections. Indeed, the authoritarian regime implemented since AFDL has learned to keep a hold on power despite elections. The regime obviously refuses to build institutions and a culture that go beyond a formal democracy based on selective elections.

Two electoral terms later, the actors in power still have not consolidated democracy by developing a robust set of institutions that address and monitor the vital issue of governance.

The way the National Assembly functions is telling. Indeed, instead of acting as a counterweight, this institution protects the interests of the executive and the majority of parliamentarians by simply rubber-stamping decisions. In many cases, a great number of Assembly members lack the experience, academic qualifications, motivation and understanding to address public policy issues. They are more concerned with supplementing their incomes by engaging in corrupt practices, such as selling their votes to the executive.

In such a context, the ability of democratic institutions like the parliament, the press, the armed forces, the police, the security service and the courts to play a constructive and enduring role is questionable.

It is difficult to see how they can exercise control over the government's activities and promote the reforms necessary for rebuilding the rule of law in DRC.[50]

Thus, while multiparty electoral competition seems to be the new wave, the population and especially young people are not convinced the next electoral cycle will be free and fair. What ensues from this is a mood of uncertainty, confusion and distrust among citizens. The feeling is that an alien world of political decision-makers exists separately from people's needs.

The loss of confidence in the progress and happiness promised by those in power manifests itself in the frustration and anger of the jobless literate and hungry illiterate. And unfortunately, it often ends in the resort to violence to access power or simply better social conditions and status.

---

50 The frequent failure of motions in the parliament against the prime minister and members of the government illustrates how the "mechanical majority" repeatedly says no to attempts to set out a bold national agenda for strengthening transparency and accountability for Congolese citizens.

V. Contemplating civil society's roles

The involvement of DRC civil society, the media and the population in the police reform process went through three phases.[51]

The first involved increasing the public's engagement in security sector reform. With the support of DFID, IDASA was able to support civil society engagement. Created in 2006, the *Réseau pour la r*éforme *des services de sé*curité *(*Security Services Reform Network) managed to bring the issue of security into the public domain, in spite of its organisational weaknesses. A public education programme started to emerge with the creation of citizen forums and civic education classes, thus laying the foundations for the PdP approach.

The second phase was civil society's engagement in the development of the organic law on police reform and monitoring parliamentary activity. During this phase, civil society organisations familiarised themselves with the law-making process and the security budget, via the *Groupe stratégique technique* (Technical Strategic Group). Civil society's vision for the new police service was shared with the CSRP and many of its recommendations were integrated into the draft document submitted to parliament.

The third phase involved supporting the implementation of the reforms, and thePdP concept in particular, through a bottom-up approach responsive to popular concerns.

Although it is true that the police need community assistance to maintain law and order, this aspect of the reform implementation raises challenging questions that must be tackled if a better response to Congolese people's security needs is to be achieved.

Indeed to what extent did the British Community Police or the French PdP reformers take account of how Congolese people have themselves provided security and imposed law and order in various contexts where the state's presence is either limited or has totally collapsed?

Is it true that the British or French approach will meet the diverse expectations of different Congolese communities in Western and Eastern Congo? Could we not do with a bottom-up approach that promotes a flexible, cheaper system to meet people's security needs; a system that will be sustainable and easily appropriated by the communities?

These are the kinds of questions the RRSSJ should continue debating in

---

51 Interesting data sets are now available. See RRSS office and the EA-SSAPR project. Kinshasa, DR Congo.

the course of the complex implementation process. Relevant responses to these issues will certainly promote a state police reform approach that relies on local, not ethnic, police initiatives that are integrated into a regulatory and normative national framework. Such a process will hopefully address the issue of popular ownership of the reform project and secure community-specific initiatives.

V.1. a new citizenship for a different police

In Congo, inventing a new citizenship for a new police is a must. Although insignificant, efforts in this direction are already under way. They explain the present resistance to any repressive authoritarian police and the people's thirst for a "public service" police.

Now, various civil society organisations and police officers are saying "no": "no" to a conception of police that does not place the human being at its core; no, to political agreements outlining reforms that do not consider the will of the people who suffer; no, to our fears that prevent people from recovering the courage, joys and pleasures of individual and collective commitment to reforms from below that promote human dignity.

It is not superfluous to insist that Congolese rulers take up the challenge of rethinking the police establishment in this rapidly changing social environment. It is important to question the why's of police ways of thinking and acting.

The plea is to avoid new confrontations. The purpose is to create a context in which both police and population set out on a common search for new roles for police institutions that restore human dignity. Obviously it is no easy task.

Restoring the balance between police and population is primarily a question of rebuilding a relationship. It is a matter of abandoning the destructive relationship whereby the police see themselves as subjects and the ruled population as objects. The aim is to create a civil-police relationship based on "actors", on partners who exchange, who do not take without giving.

V.2. Debating civil-police relations

The Congolese population suffers all forms of abuse, intimidation and harassment at the hands of security forces, which believe they are all powerful and treat citizens with complete disdain. Most conflicts between populace and police are the result of police failure to assist those in danger, usurpation of power, extortion, corruption, arbitrary arrest, illegal detention, etc.

The historical evolution of the police force is partly responsible for this situation. Under colonial rule, militia groups were trained to tame, repress and punish those who would not submit to the colonial authorities. Civilians were looked down upon as animals: "*civil azalimusenzi, civil bilangaya soda!*" ("Civilians are savages; civilians are the fields we weed!").

These beliefs still influence police practices today. The population is fearful and scornful of security agents and the services they represent. Citizens, mostly students, have invented many nicknames for police officers. A policeman is a "*waya-waya*", "the one who never smiles before pay-day", "service number 00", "the corrupt accomplice who is quick to release criminals", etc.

This disdain is also reflected in the fact that families never allow their brightest children to enter the police force. But is the promotion of a "police public service" conceivable if Congolese families refuse to send the best of their children into the police?

The need to improve police-civil relations is certainly at the centre of the current police reform process. The intent is to develop another style of civil-police relations and encourage local-level responsibility.

The police academy is a joint training institution that can bring civilians and police personnel together, at least for short-term courses of three or six months. Such courses can allow professionals from different backgrounds to build a teamwork tradition in the field of police and security.

The establishment of interdepartmental security committees on issues such as food supplies, scientific research, health and environmental security is also a way of ensuring a healthy civil-police relationship.[52] At the head of each committee there should be a civilian, thus expressing in concrete terms the subordination of the police to civil control.

To facilitate a positive civil-police dialogue on security issues, police institutions ought to be opened to civilians to allow them access to police facilities insights into the realities of policing. Sports competitions can also build civil-police trust.

Successful civil-police relations require the gradual creation of a new horizontal relationship, different from the vertical model of today. In the new

---

52 A challenging EA-SSAPR programme initiative (2012) is intended to train Congolese researchers on security issues and reduce the wide gap between locally and externally generated knowledge. The key aim is to enhance the expertise of Congolese actors working on and advocating improvements in security and justice provision, rather than to simply produce information for publication. This strategy will, it is hoped, promote a positive civil-police dialogue.

relationship, there is no superior on one side and subordinate on the other. Rather, we will discover police officers collaborating with civilians to ensure mutual protection and security. This bond is only possible if there is mutual respect, brotherhood and cooperation in restoring the peace the police and entire population need.

Civilians have an obligation to develop monitoring and evaluation mechanisms for police behaviour and actions. Citizen control or better "participatory governance" is a procedure whereby citizens participate in the management of public affairs.

This approach implies that the beneficiaries, namely the populace, ask rulers to account for their conduct. This citizen oversight is undertaken in respect of the constitution and laws of the republic. In this case, civil society structures (NGOs, church organisations, cultural associations, trade unions, women's associations, etc.) control the quality of the services provided by the police

To reach this goal, mechanisms and techniques must be developed and implemented within civil society organisations. Among these mechanisms and techniques, the most appropriate are observation and fact analysis, advocacy and lobbying, information, monitoring and evaluation.

All these approaches aim at giving effect to popular supervision of police services. They will hopefully help change the attitudes of both police officers and the populace towards one another and improve security conditions.

Assessment of popular attitudes can be done through the popular expression forums, opinion polls and suggestion boxes in police stations and substations. The purpose of such assessments is the improvement of service based on objectively verifiable indicators.

VI. Measuring effects

The aim of most internal or external evaluations of the PdP reform process has been to provide information about the relevance and effects of police reform so as to inform decisions about the future of the programme and update external partners in the process.

So far, reform evaluation has been concerned with contextual analysis, mapping strategic framework (logframe and workplan), programme relevance and impacts, programme cost effectiveness, assessment of research contributions and appraisal of support for implementation and policy development on programme outcomes

Debates with SSAPR monitoring and evaluation experts involved in project assessment have drawn attention to the police reform project's limited systematic measuring and reporting of impacts and progress indicators. M&E experts regularly insisted on the need to develop evaluation tools that measure the outputs and outcomes of police reform in a comprehensive and informative way.

Unfortunately, this programme failed for many reasons that remain obscure. However, the failure probably confirms the complexity of elaborating such instruments in an environment lacking in data that document present police reform wins or losses or drawing attention to a number of conditions essential for the reform success.

Obviously, notwithstanding the political and financial investment in the police reconstruction effort, no systematic impact measures were developed in advance to recognise negative developments and to document progress during the reform process.[53] According to M&E experts, common data such as number of police officers trained, vehicles supplied, amount of equipment provided, number of workshops organised were not reliable, systematic and comprehensive evaluation tools.

Indeed, several years after the initiation of the reform process, these tools still have not changed the general impression among internal and external reformers that reform efforts have had almost no impact, since they are unable to capture the outcomes of police reform. Their analyses questioned assessments that relied only on a mixture of anecdote, frequent technical exercises such as log frames and workplan revisions and ad hoc reports.

---

53 Conversation with SSAPR M&E programme experts, DR Congo. Interesting insights can be found in Loh (2010), pp. 20–44.

In consequence, the absence of documented impact of the reform process in its first steps has led to great disappointment. This dearth of information and reports on initial improvements does not help in attempts to convince internal and external reformers to stay committed.

VII. to conclude: what next?

Even if wish-lists remain in the realm of the "somewhat possible", experts very often present lists based on realistic demands that soon become unrealistic demands. This is because they do not dare to end the ostrich policy that, for so-called diplomatic reasons, constantly avoids significant efforts to address basic governance issues that stand in the way of the unfolding police reform process .

Indeed, police reform would have operated within a more constructive context if only the international community had responded differently to the flawed elections of 2011. A firm stand would have established the vital link between regime legitimacy and the strong political backing needed for various crucial reforms.

Today, internal and external reformers are eager to see what level of commitment the regime that emerged from the fraudulent elections will provide a reform process that needs a strong driver to overcome institutional, formal and informal resistance.

In this regard, it is probably better to list the questions that still haunt reformers and reform beneficiaries, instead of drawing up a valid wish-list that, unfortunately, the present weak political environment cannot deliver on.

Indeed, does the expected strong driver of reform have the moral resources to impose reform and survive politically? To what extent can the president and his comrades accept reform that will weaken their grip on power? What reform can police reformers obtain from a regime, which even though it was elected "democratically", is vulnerable to attempted coups? What can reformers expect from leaders and a government that emerged from messy compromises and peace deals and therefore feels obliged to retain strong control over the police and security sector? Are reformers aware of the capacity of various local actors (ethnic, tribal, local, regional, sub-regional, political, economic, racial, etc.) to obstruct and undermine reform? What can reformers expect of a parliament whose ability to play a constructive and enduring role is questionable? And finally, how can both reform providers and recipients change the police in the absence of wider state reforms?

Only a democratic state with a brave and decisive leadership and legitimate power deriving from governance and the rule of law can answer the above questions with suggestions that may be challenging, but which belong in realm of the "actually possible".

Successful police and other reforms to come require recognition of the need to move away from a state that relies on the liberation ethos to a state that avoids legitimising apparatuses without real power and unable to undertake successful police reform.

Although no stimulating answers have been provided at the present stage of the reform process, I suggest we keep the questions raised in this study in mind to understand where we stand today on the eve of implementing police reform. I sincerely hope these questions will not quench internal and external reformers' enthusiasm but will alert them not to do what they have done in past police reforms, and thereby repeat the endless cycle of failed reforms.

Bibliography

Africa Progress Panel (2013) "Equity in Extractives: Stewarding Africa's Natural Resources for All". Africa Progress Report. Geneva.

African Movement of Grassroots non-State Organizations (2009) "Une analyse des expériences non-étatiques de police de proximité en RDC". Geneva Centre for the Democratic Control of Armed Forces Working Paper No 17. *www.IPES. Info.www.dcaf.ch. International Police Executive.*

Albrecht, P. (2010) "Transforming Internal Security in Sierra Leone: Sierra Leone Police and Broader Justice Sector Reform". Danish Institute for International Studies Report No. 7. Copenhagen.

Congolese Constitution (18 February 2006) and Organic Law n°08/016 (7 October 2008). In *Journal officiel de la République Démocratique du Congo* (10 octobre 2008), *Numéro spécial*, 49me année. Kinshasa.

Doss A., J. Herbst and G. Mills (2013) "Armed Forces in Contemporary Africa: Towards a Taxonomy of Militaries?" In *A Dialogue on the African Military in an Age of Democracy*. Tswalu Kalahari Reserve, 22-24 February, p.9.

Doyle, M. (1999) "British Clean-up for Sierra Leone Police". *BBC News,* Thursday 25 November, http://news.bbc.co.uk/1/hi/world/Africa/536233.stm

Ebenga J. and T. Nlandu (2005) "The Congolese National Army.In Search of an Identity". In M. Rupiya (ed), *Evolutions and Revolutions: A Contemporary Africa*. Pretoria: Institute for Security Studies.

Ericksson Baaz M. and J. Verweijen (2013a) "The Volatility of a Half-Cooked Bouillabaisse.Rebel-Military integration and Conflict Dynamics in Eastern DRC. African Affairs". Draft, July.

Ericksson Baaz M. (2013) "Between Integration and Disintegration: The Erratic Trajectory of the Congolese Army". Draft paper for Social Science Research Council.

Ericksson Baaz. M. and M. Stern (2013b) *Sexual Violence as a Weapon of War? Perceptions, Problems in the Congo and Beyond.* Uppsala and London: Nordiska Afrikainstitutet and Zed Books.

GMRRR Final Report (2006) *www.reformedelapnc.org/documents/GMRRR_Report-en-Francais.pdf; www.reformedelapnc.org.*

GMRRR PNC (2007) "Travaux de réflexion sur la réforme de la Police Nationale Congolaise". Ministère de l'Intérieur, Décentralisation et Sécurité. DR Congo.

Justaert, A. (2011) "The Governance of Police reform in the DRC: Reformwithout Alignment?". 4th European Conference on African Studies, African Engagements: On Whose Terms?". Uppsala,15–18 June.

Kabila, L. (2011) Inaugural Speech. In *Bulletin d'Information sur la réforme de la police. Bulletin* n°0.CSRP.*www.csrp.cd. CSRP.* DR Congo.

Loh J. (2010) "Success Factors for Police Reform in Post-conflict Situations". Hertie School of Governance Working Papers. No. 57, pp. 20–44.

Mayambula Nkoyi-Sweswe, A. (2012) "Rapport du Monitoring de la prestation de Policiers dans le Commissariat et Sous commissariats de Référence de la Commune de Nzanza". Matadi, DR Congo, October.

Nlandu Mayamba. T. (2000) "When Illiterates and Literates Move Beyond Political Democracy". *Http//i-p-o-org/congdem 2.htm*

Nlandu Mayamba. T. (2006) "Autopsie de la société civile congolaise". In [editor?], *Du Zaïre au Congo Démocratique. Une plume pour une transition en folie?* Paris: Publibook.

Nlandu Mayamba, T. (2012a) "La rébellion du M23: une rébellion de façade et d'un cynisme qui interpelle les Congolais?" www.ingeta.com

Nlandu Mayamba, T. (2012b) "Module de formation sur la police". Draft. Composante Redevabilité Externe. Programme d'appui à la redevabilité du secteur de sécurité et la réforme de la Police en République Démocratique du Congo. DAI, DR Congo.

Nlandu Mayamba, T. (2012c) "Mapping Police Services in the Democratic Republic of Congo: Institutional Interactions at Central, Provincial and Local Levels". IDS Research Report 71. Institute of Development Studies, London.

Nsaka-Kabunda. A.M. (2011) "La réforme de la Police Nationale Congolaise. Contribution des partenairesinternationaux".*www.the rule of law in Africa*.com/wp content/uploads/

Obasanjo, O., D. Richards, L Dias Diogo and R. Myers (2013) "The Changing Role of Armies in the Age of Democracy". In *Business Day,* 11 March.

OECD (2004) "Security System Reform and Governance: Policy and Good Practice. A DCAF Reference Document". Paris: Organisation for Economic Cooperation and Development.

RCN Justice et Démocratie (2010) "Les systèmes locaux de sécurité et de justice en République Démocratique du Congo. Etude de cas dans les provinces du Bas-Congo, du Kasaï Occidental et du Sud Kivu. Etude sur les systèmes locaux de sécurité et de justice". Kinshasa.

UN Secretary General (30 March 2010) 31st Secretary General Report. §44, *www. un.org*

Utas. M. (2012) "Introduction: Bigmanity and Network Governance in African Conflicts". In [author/editor?], *African Conflicts and Informal Power: Big Men and Networks*. London and New York: Zed Books.

Van Woudenberg A. and B. Shepherd (2013) Transcript: "What Next for the Democratic Republic of the Congo?" 20 February. *www.chathamhouse.org 2*

Wolters S. (2004) "Update on the DRC: Is the Transition in Trouble?" *ISS Situation Report*. Pretoria: Institute for Security Studies.

Yamba Tshintu, C. (2012) "Les programmes DDR et DDRRR: état des lieux des opérations et propositions pour l'avenir". In [author/editor?], *Atelier national sur "Les enjeux sécuritaires en RDC : quels axes pour une paix durable?"*. Kinshasa, RD Congo.

www.ingramcontent.com/pod-product-compliance
Lightning Source LLC
Chambersburg PA
CBHW070817280326
41934CB00012B/3215